Crashproof your BBC

Crashproof your BBC

Software Tips for
BBC and Electron Programs

Mike McNamara

JOHN WILEY & SONS
Chichester · New York · Brisbane · Toronto · Singapore

Copyright ©1984 by John Wiley & Sons Ltd

All rights reserved.

No part of this book may be reproduced by any means, nor transmitted, nor translated into a machine language without the written permission of the publisher

Library of Congress Cataloging in Publication Data:

McNamara, Mike.
   Crashproof your BBC.

   Includes index.
   1. BBC Microcomputer. I. Title. II. Title:
Crashproof your B.B.C.
QA76.8.B35M36   1984   001,64   84-17343
ISBN 0 471 90609 3

British Library Cataloguing in Publication Data:

McNamara, Mike
   Crashproof your BBC.
   1. BBC Microcomputer
   I. Title
   001.64'04   QA76.8.B35

   ISBN 0 471 90609 3

Typeset by Pintail Studios, Ringwood, Hampshire.
Printed in Great Britain by Page Bros., Norwich.

Contents

The Book (Introduction)	1
The BREAK Key	5
The ESCAPE Key	17
Hints and Tips	29
Use of Tapes	31
Sound OFF	32
Auto Repeat OFF/ON	33
Cursor and Copy Keys OFF/ON	35
Clear the Function Keys	36
Dropping the Screen Display	37

Randomize	38
Flashing Cursor OFF	40
Shift and Caps Lock ON/OFF	41
Keyboard OFF/ON	43
Flush the Keyboard Buffer	44
Index (An INDEX Program)	47
INDEX Listing	50
Auto Boot	55
Back-up Copies	59

The Book

During the summer of 1983 I ran a short summer school in computing for primary-aged children. To help me run the course I enlisted the aid of a number of local primary teachers and interested parents. My hopes for the course were twofold:

1. That the children would gain experience of the computers in a relaxed and fun atmosphere.
2. That the teachers, who had volunteered to help, would gain valuable experience in the use of computers with children.

My role was to act as the course 'expert' since:

   a. I am a teacher.

   b. I had, at the time, had over 2 years experience in the use of the BBC microcomputer.

It was as the course was running that the need for this book came to light.

Each day various problems would arise with the software in use. The kids would be working away and suddenly everything stopped, or the screen went blank. A call of panic would go up and I would get called over. The usual comments would be:

'The program won't work!'

or

'The computer's gone wrong!'

In fact 9 times out of 10 the answer was simply that the software had not been designed well enough to cope with inexperienced users. Thus, in most cases I was able to spot the fault and rapidly get the program going again.

It was this that raised comments. The adults standing watching would ask, 'How on earth did you do that?', so I would explain it to them and out would come pen and paper.

I started to think about where I had found the solutions myself. I realized that most had come from my attempts to produce software for the classroom. Many were found through trial and error and a few from friends.

Hence this book. It is simply an attempt to bring the more useful solutions together in one place.

I hope that you will find it of use and that it may provide solutions to at least a few of your problems.

Thanks

At this point I would like to thank those people who gave their advice and encouragement during the production of this book. In particular I would like to thank Mr David Bell and Mr David Barnard, for their advice on the book, and the staff of Castlehurst Ltd at Whetstone, for allowing me to test the commands on the Electron.

BREAK

Location: Top right of the keyboard.

The BREAK key on the BBC microcomputer is designed to stop the computer, no matter what it is doing at the time. In addition it causes the computer to 'forget' all that it has been set to do.

Hence pressing the BREAK key is a rather drastic action. As a general rule its use should be avoided as much as possible. It is also advisable to warn (or ask) all users not to press it.

However, when it comes to inquisitive users, the word BREAK on a key acts as an almost irresistible magnet to their fingers. This makes it virtually certain that it will be pressed, no matter what they are told.

What then does this key do and how can its impact be reduced?

When you switch on the BBC microcomputer you will get a message on the screen:

DISC BASED   **TAPE BASED**

BBC Computer 32K   **BBC Computer 32K**
Acorn DFS   **BASIC**
BASIC   >_
>_

When you switch on the Electron you will get the message:

Acorn Electron
BASIC
>_

If, while a program is being run on the computer the BREAK key is pressed, and its effects have not been guarded against, the above messages return to the screen. Trying to RUN the program again will fail, as will trying to LIST the program. It therefore appears that the program has been lost. In most cases you can find that elusive program and drag it out of its hiding place by entering the following:

OLD <RETURN>
RUN <RETURN>

The program should now be back and working as normal. But remember, any work that was done before the BREAK key was pressed will have been lost.

Unfortunately, some programs have heavy copyright protection or are stored in the computer in odd ways. With such programs pressing the BREAK key destroys part or all of the program and the above recovery technique will only result in the message: 'Bad program'. In these cases your only option is to reload the program from its tape or disc (with luck you were using discs!).

Obviously, if you are trying to get people to use the computer who have little or no experience, then it would be desirable for you to be able to reduce the impact of the BREAK key in some way. I say reduce since the BREAK key cannot be turned off. The BBC microcomputer provides a number of options which can enable us to do this. Hopefully, one of these options will suit your particular needs.

Option 1: (BBC & Electron)

*KEY 10 OLD¦M RUN¦M

The symbol ¦ can be found just to the right of and below the BREAK key on the BBC, and on the key to the left of the BREAK key on the Electron. On the screen it appears as a ǁ. It is accessed through the SHIFT key.

This rather odd looking line has the same effect as entering OLD and RUN after the BREAK key has been pressed.

*KEY 10 refers to the BREAK key.
OLD¦M has the same effect as OLD <RETURN>
RUN¦M has the same effect as RUN <RETURN>
(¦M has the same effect as pressing RETURN)

The easiest way of using this option is to do the following:

1. **LOAD the program using LOAD"name"**
2. **Enter the line *KEY 10 OLD¦M RUN¦M**
3. **RUN the program.**

If you press the BREAK key now, the screen will go blank for a second. The original start-up screen message will flash up, and then the program will rerun from the start. In other words pressing the BREAK key will now automatically OLD and RUN the program for you.

The main drawback of this particular option is that it needs to be repeated every time you use the program. This is rather slow and clumsy, and many people may find it rather confusing.

Option 2: (BBC & Electron)

This option also relies on the use of the line:

*KEY 10 OLD!M RUN!M

However, in this case we will build it into the program to be protected, so that every time you use the program the BREAK key is automatically rendered less harmful.

To do this will require some work on the program itself. DON'T PANIC, this is not as hard as you may think!

1. **LOAD the program to be protected, using LOAD"name".**
2. **Enter RENUMBER <RETURN>**
3. **Now type:**

   5 *KEY 10 OLD!M RUN!M

and press RETURN
*4. **Now you will need to SAVE the new version of the program with its protection. To do this you use:**

   SAVE"name" <RETURN>

Note: RENUMBERing the program before entering the *KEY 10 line makes quite sure that line 5 is free for use.

*For a more detailed explanation of program saving see the section on the production of 'Back-up copies'.

Both options 1 and 2 have a major drawback. As soon as BREAK is pressed the program starts again from the beginning, without providing any explanation to the user as to what has occurred. The next option still uses *KEY 10 but in such a way as to provide an explanation to the user as to what has happened.

Option 3: (BBC & Electron)

To provide an explanation we again need to add to the existing program.

1. LOAD the program into the computer.
2. RENUMBER the program as in option 2.
3. LIST the program and make a note of the last line number.
4. Enter the line:

   5 *KEY 10 OLD!M GOTO x !M

   where x is 10 greater than the last line number.

e.g.

```
5 *KEY 10 OLD:M GOTO 1250:M
10 Beginning of the programme
:
:
:
1240 End of the programme
```

You then add the following to the end of the program:

```
1250 CLS
1260 PRINT TAB(10,5);"You have pressed the"
1270 PRINT TAB(16);"BREAK key."
1280 PRINT TAB(12,10);"This has stopped"
1290 PRINT TAB(13);"the programme."
1300 PRINT TAB(14,15);"Press any key"
1310 PRINT TAB(13);"to start again."
1320 GO$=GET$
1330 RUN
```

Once this has been added and the program has been run, pressing the BREAK key will result in the message appearing on the screen. Pressing any key will then rerun the program. In this way the user is not simply dumped back at the beginning without warning, but is informed of their action.

Having added these lines to the end of your program you will need to SAVE a new version of the program.

So far all of the options explained have been designed to keep and rerun the program currently in use. All three will work equally well with both tape- and disc-based systems.

The following options are designed for those people who are using disc-based systems.

Option 4: (BBC Only)

For this option to work you will first need to have set up an INDEX program on your disc. If you do not already have an INDEX program then you will find one listed in this book.

To set up this option you will need to:

1. **LOAD the program to be protected.**
2. **RENUMBER the program to free line 5.**
3. **Enter the following line:**

    5 *KEY 10 CHAIN"INDEX"|M

4. **SAVE your new program.**

In this way, when you use the new program, pressing the BREAK key will result in the LOADing and RUNning of your INDEX program.

I.e. The BREAK key, far from being a problem, has become the access key to the rest of your programs.

However, we are still left with some programs which, for one reason or another, cannot be 'got at' in any of the ways yet described. My final option will provide a means by which disc users can overcome this problem.

Option 5: (BBC Only)

Before you can set up this option you will require two additional elements:

a. An INDEX program.
b. Your disc set up to AUTO BOOT the INDEX program.

N.B. Full details on these can be found in this book.

Whereas all of the previous options have involved additions to the program you wish to protect, this option requires the addition of one line to your INDEX program.

1. **LOAD your INDEX program.**
2. **RENUMBER the INDEX program.**
3. **Add the following line:**

   5 *FX255,7

4. **SAVE your new INDEX program.**

Note: Normally the AUTO BOOT system is obtained by pressing BREAK and SHIFT together, and then releasing them, BREAK first.

Once the command *FX255,7 has been given

however, an AUTO BOOT can be obtained by pressing the BREAK key alone. Thus, no matter what the program currently running, pressing BREAK will result in your INDEX program being loaded and run.

ESCAPE

Location: Top left of the keyboard,
to the left of the
number one key.

The ESCAPE key on the BBC microcomputer has been designed to stop the program the computer is running. However, it will leave the program being used intact. It may also be programmed to do other jobs if required.

Thus, if the unprotected ESCAPE key is pressed, the program running will be stopped. In addition a message is displayed on the screen, e.g.

Escape at line 50

or

Escape at line 1230

After ESCAPE has been pressed the program can be restarted simply by entering the command RUN and pressing <RETURN>. This unfortunately starts the program from the very beginning, and any work done will need to be re-entered.

However, pressing ESCAPE does not cause the computer to 'forget' what it has been doing. Because of this it is sometimes possible to get the program to restart from where you ESCAPEd by entering the following:

GOTO *n* where *n* is the number given in the ESCAPE message. E.g.

Message: Escape at line 120
Enter: GOTO 120 <RETURN>

Unfortunately, the program often stops again very quickly since ESCAPE was pressed during a program loop or procedure. If this occurs then simply return to the original solution, i.e. RUN <RETURN>

However, it is worth a try since, when it does work,

no data is lost and the program continues from where it left off.

Since pressing ESCAPE does not cause the computer to forget what it has been doing, many programs actually use the ESCAPE key to carry out a specific job.

For example, it may be used to 'Freeze' the action or send the current screen to a printer. In this type of program the ESCAPE key does not present a problem to the user. In many other programs however, the ESCAPE key poses most definite problems to the user. It is with the latter program types in mind that the following information is given.

* Option 1: (BBC & Electron)

The ESCAPE key is probably most dangerous when the program running requires a large amount of numeric entry. It is all too easy to press ESCAPE by mistake, when trying to press the number 1.

The easiest solution is to switch the ESCAPE key off. This can be done in the following way:

1. **LOAD the program.**
2. **Enter:**

    *FX 200,1 <RETURN>

3. **RUN the program.**

Pressing the ESCAPE key after this will have no effect at all.

* Option 2: (BBC & Electron)

Build *FX 200,1 into the program as a permanent feature.

1. **LOAD the program.**
2. **RENUMBER the program.**
3. **Enter:**

    5 *FX 200,1 <RETURN>

4. **SAVE the new program.**

   * These options will only work if the Operating System of the computer is a 1.0 or above. They do not work on the old 0.1 system. To find out which you have simply enter:

*FX 0 <RETURN>

If you find that you have the old 0.1 system then you can use:

*FX 220,0

This does not switch the ESCAPE key off, but disables

it. Thus when pressed it will not stop the program. However, it does return the value 27. In some cases this may still cause problems in a program.

* Option 3: (BBC & Electron)

Since the danger of the Escape key is due to its closeness to the number 1, a useful option is to 'move' the Escape key. In fact, moving the Escape key means transferring the Escape function to another key. This is done by using the command:

*FX 220,*n*

Here *n* is the code number of the key you wish to act as Escape.
　For example:

*FX 220,9 (BBC Only)

This will move the Escape action to the TAB key (code 9).

*FX 220,0

This will move the Escape function to <CTRL>-@, i.e pressing <CTRL> and @ together gives an Escape.

*FX 220,176

This will give the Escape action with

<SHIFT>-<CTRL>-f0. Thus, three keys need to be pressed together to give an Escape.

*FX220,91 (Electron)

This gives an Escape from a <SHIFT>-<COPY>.

As with the *FX 200,*n* option in 1 and 2 above, these commands can either be entered before the program is run, or they can be built in as a permanent feature.

The BBC microcomputer has a rather odd looking command:

ON ERROR

This is designed to change the way the computer responds to errors in a program. However, it can also be used to detect the pressing of the ESCAPE key. It can therefore be used to overcome some of the problems of pressing ESCAPE.

Option 4: (BBC & Electron)

As with the *FX in options 1 and 2 above, this can be implemented in two ways:

1. (i) **LOAD the program.**
   (ii) **Enter:**

   ON ERROR RUN <RETURN>

   (iii) **RUN the program.**

2. (i) **LOAD the program.**
   (ii) **RENUMBER the program.**
   (iii) **Enter:**

   5 ON ERROR RUN <RETURN>

   (iv) **SAVE the new program.**

Whichever method is used, pressing ESCAPE will now result in the program starting again automatically.

This can be very useful when a program is to be used by several people. Each new user simply presses ESCAPE to start the program again.

Option 5: (BBC & Electron)

This again uses the ON ERROR command. In this case however, a message is given to the user. Thus the user knows what they have done and is invited to start again.

1. **LOAD the program.**
2. **RENUMBER the program.**
3. **LIST the program and make a note of the last line number.**
4. **Enter the line:**

    5 ON ERROR GOTO *n*

    where *n* is 10 greater that the last line number. e.g.

```
5 ON ERROR GOTO 2010
10 Beginning of the programme
:
:
:
2000 Last line of programme
```

5. Add the following to the end of the program:

A.

```
2010 MODE 7
2020 PRINT TAB(10,5);"You have pressed the"
2030 PRINT TAB(15);"ESCAPE key."
2040 PRINT TAB(12,10);"This has stopped"
2050 PRINT TAB(13);"the programme."
2060 PRINT TAB(14,15);"Press any key"
2070 PRINT TAB(13);"to start again."
2080 GO$=GET$
2090 CLEAR
2100 RUN
```

or

B.

```
2010 MODE 7
2020 PRINT TAB(8,10);"Please tell your teacher"
2030 PRINT TAB(8);"that you have finished."
2040 GO$=GET$
2050 IF GO$ = "@" THEN 2070
2060 GOTO 2040
2070 CLEAR
2080 RUN
```

In A above pressing ESCAPE will result in the message being given. Then pressing any key will result in the program restarting.

In B above the message will be given after an ESCAPE but the program can only be restarted by pressing the @ key.

In both cases replace the MODE 7 command with MODE 6 if using the Electron.

Hints & Tips

This chapter of the book deals with the idea of program protection. By this I do not mean finding ways of preventing people copying the programs. Instead I refer to methods of protection which can be used to reduce the risks of a user causing a program to fail (or crash).

In this chapter a selection of short commands will be given and explained. These commands provide a wide selection of 'protective' features for software used by non-computer experts.

In most cases the commands can either be entered before the program is run, or can be built into the program as a permanent feature. In each case the various options will be given, and their implementation explained. In addition to these protective features I have also included a number of other features which I feel may be of general help.

Ideally, any software being produced for commercial sale should contain all appropriate protection before it is put on the market. However, this is not, at present, the case. All too often basically good software is spoiled by the absence of such simple protection.

If you are willing and able to add the protection yourself then you may not feel that this is too serious. If you do not feel up to making additions to your software, or the software is protected to prevent you from doing so, then why not send it back to the producers with recommendations for its improvement?

Even if you can make the changes, I am sure that most software writers would be more than pleased to hear your constructive suggestions.

1. Use of Tapes: (BBC Only)

One problem with the BBC microcomputer is that it is rather short of memory. To make matters worse, if you are using a disc-based system an extra chunk of memory is lost. This is because the computer sets it aside for the disc system. Thus, if you are using tape-based software this memory can be lost and wasted. In some cases this may result in the program failing to run due to a lack of memory. To overcome this problem do the following BEFORE loading the tape-based software:

1. Enter: *TAPE <RETURN>
2. Enter: PAGE=&E00 <RETURN>

This will 'grab back' the memory that the computer was setting aside for the discs you are not using.

Once you have entered these commands you proceed to load the software in the normal way. i.e.

CHAIN"name" <RETURN>

N.B. Once the above has been done the BREAK key must NOT be pressed. If it is the computer will 'grab back' the section of memory you acquired and the program will be lost.

2. Sound OFF: (BBC & Electron)

Many pieces of software use the BBC microcomputer's ability to produce sound. In some situations these sound effects can prove very disruptive. It is therefore useful to be able to switch the sound off. This can be done in the following way:

1. **Enter: *FX 210,1 <RETURN>**
2. **CHAIN the program.**

In most cases this will result in the sound output of the computer being stopped. However, it should be noted that, in some cases the program switches it back on.

3. Auto Repeat OFF/ON: (BBC & Electron)

On the BBC microcomputer if a key is pressed and held down it enters an auto repeat sequence. Thus a whole string of characters can be produced. People not experienced in the use of a keyboard are prone to holding keys down longer than needed. To prevent this happening in a piece of software we can use:

***FX 11,0**

A. Temporary fix:
   i. **Enter: *FX11,0 <RETURN>**
   ii. **CHAIN the program.**

B. Permanent fix:
   i. **LOAD the program.**
   ii. **RENUMBER the program.**
   iii. **Enter: 5 *FX 11,0 <RETURN>**
   iv. **SAVE the new version.**

To switch the auto repeat on again use:

***FX 12,0**

There is no simple answer as to where you would

put this command. This is due to the fact that it is different in each program. It is therefore up to the user to find the appropriate place in the program for the command.

4. Cursor and Copy Keys OFF/ON: (BBC & Electron)

In many programs the cursor and copy keys have no function. However, if they are pressed by mistake they can spoil the display and cause confusion. For this reason you may wish to switch them off. To do this:

A. Temporary fix:
   i. **Enter: *FX 4,6 <RETURN>**
   ii. **CHAIN the program.**

B. Permanent fix:
   i. **LOAD the program.**
   ii. **RENUMBER the program.**
   iii. **Enter: 5 *FX 4,6 <RETURN>**
   iv. **SAVE the new version.**

To return the action of the cursor and copy keys to normal you use:

*FX 4,0 <RETURN>

Again the exact location of this command depends on the program in question.

5. Clear the Function Keys: (BBC & Electron)

Many programs use the red function keys of the BBC microcomputer to carry out a range of operations. If during a period of use a number of programs are run which use these keys problems may occur. To remove any risk the computer offers the command:

*FX 18

This clears all of the function keys so leaving them ready for later use.

This command can be placed either within each program to be used or, if a disc system is being used, within the disc INDEX program. Generally, the latter location is preferable since it only requires the addition of the command to one program per disc.

In either case the command is implemented in the same way:

i. **LOAD the program.**
ii. **RENUMBER the program.**
iii. **Enter: 5 *FX 18 <RETURN>**
iv. **SAVE the new version.**

6. Dropping the Screen Display: (BBC Only)

Quite often it is found that the top line of the screen display is too high for it to be seen. If this is the case then the display needs to be dropped by one or two lines. To do this use the command:

*TV *n*
*TV 255: drops the display by one line.
*TV 254: drops the display by two lines.
*TV 253: drops the display by three lines.

However, before these commands have any effect the screen mode must be changed, i.e. to drop the display by one line enter:

i. ***TV 255 <RETURN>**
ii. **MODE 7 <RETURN>**
iii. **CHAIN the program.**

7. Randomize: (Only tested on BBC)

In many programs selections are made by the computer on a 'random' basis, e.g. the selection of numbers in a maths program. To do this the BBC microcomputer uses the command RND(*n*), where *n* is the maximum number size. However, this selection is not truly random. This is due to the fact that the numbers are selected from a pre-set list of random numbers. Thus, when RND is used it takes the next number in the list. As a result, regular use of a program may reveal a pattern. To overcome this problem and make the selection more random we can use:

Q% = RND(−TIME)

This rather strange line has the effect of setting the selection of numbers to a random point in the list.

Since this is a rather difficult command to remember, it is best built into the program.

i. **LOAD the program.**
ii. **RENUMBER the program.**
iii. **Enter: 5 Q% = RND(−TIME) <RETURN>**
iv. **SAVE the new version.**

If the program is protected in such a way as to make

this impossible then:

i. **Enter: Q% = RND(–TIME) <RETURN>**
ii. **CHAIN the program.**

8. Flashing Cursor OFF: (BBC & Electron)

The BBC microcomputer prompts the user to enter data with a small flashing line or cursor. In some situations this flashing cursor really is a curse. It can be very distracting and may even spoil the display. This need not be the case since it can be switched off. To do this we use the command:

VDU 23;8202;0;0;0;

or

VDU 23;11,0;0;0;0 (BBC Only)

However, in each case the cursor will be switched back on again as soon as the program changes screen mode. Thus to use this command you must be able to find out where the program changes mode. Once you have found the mode changes (there may well be more than one), either of the above commands can be added after it. E.g.

40 MODE 7
45 VDU 23;8202;0;0;0;

9. Shift and Caps Lock ON/OFF: (BBC Only)

Another feature of the BBC microcomputer that can be controlled from within a program as well as through the keyboard is the control of the caps and shift locks.

Functions:

Both OFF: Lower case letters, lower symbols and numerics. Capitals and upper symbols are accessed through the SHIFT keys.

Caps lock ON: Upper case letters, lower symbols and numerics. Upper symbols accessed through the SHIFT keys.

Shift lock ON: Upper case letters and upper symbols. Numerics, lower case letters and lower symbols are not accessible.

In many programs regular input is requested. If, for example, this is for text, the program may only accept upper case entries. Due to the position of the caps and shift lock keys, it is very easy for these to be pressed, without the user knowing they have done so. This may then result in the program not accepting future entries.
    I.e.: If the program wants capitals and the caps and

shift locks are off, or if numerics are wanted and shift lock is on.

To overcome this problem additions need to be made to the program. These additions need to be inserted just before the requests for entry are made. Thus some degree of programming skill is needed. The commands to use are:

1. ***FX 202,32 caps lock ON**
2. ***FX 202,20 shift lock ON**
3. ***FX 202,50 caps and shift locks OFF**

10. Keyboard OFF/ON: (BBC & Electron)

In some programs the computer may, after an input from the user, take some time to calculate and display its response. During this delay many users, not sure of what is happening, press several keys. When the program resumes you may well find that odd things occur. This is due to the fact that the computer has remembered the keys pressed, and is now acting upon them. To prevent this from happening the keyboard can be switched off for the calculation period.

The command used to switch the keyboard off is:

*FX 201,1

To switch it back on again use:

*FX 201,0

Unfortunately, the exact location within a program, for these commands, depends on the program.

11. Flush the Keyboard Buffer: (BBC & Electron)

When you press a key on the computer the code of the key is stored in the keyboard buffer until the computer is ready to use it. Thus, the keyboard buffer fills with a queue of codes for the computer. Normally this is of no consequence to the user and can be ignored. However, in some situations it can cause problems.

For example: a program may begin with a series of introduction 'pages'. To move from one to the next you are asked to press the SPACE BAR. If you press the space bar more than once (by mistake or due to over-enthusiasm) you may well miss one of the 'pages'. This may well provide problems later in the program.

To prevent such a problem we need to 'clean out' or flush the stored codes. This is done using the command:

*FX 21,0

This is best located just before any request for input in the program. Thus its exact location depends on the program concerned.

As a final point, it should be noted that in some cases the methods given may not work. If this should occur then the following may help.

Before any attempt to load the program is made, enter the protective code you require.

For example: you have a program called 'COUNT' which requires the ESCAPE and BREAK keys to be protected and for the keyboard auto repeat to be switched off. The program is written in such a way as to prevent you using the methods already given. To provide the protection wanted do the following:

Enter:

a. ***KEY10 OLD!M RUN!M <RETURN>**
b. ***FX 200,1 <RETURN>**
c. ***FX 11,0 <RETURN>**
d. **CHAIN "COUNT" <RETURN>**

In this way the protection is set up before the program is loaded and run. However, you may still find problems if the program resets these values once it starts. If this is the case then the protection you want will require some reprogramming, so get in touch with the producer.

The above method of software protection can be made more permanent by the creation of a short program. Take the case as given above:

a. Enter the following program:

```
10 *KEY10 OLD|M RUN|M
20 *FX 200,1
30 *FX 11,0
40 CHAIN "COUNT"
```

b. Save this program under a new name, e.g.:

SAVE "CNT" <RETURN>

Once this has been done, instead of loading the program 'COUNT' you load the program 'CNT' by entering the command:

CHAIN "CNT" <RETURN>

In this way the small program 'CNT' will be loaded and run, so setting up the protection, and will then load and run the main program automatically.

INDEX

When using discs for program storage it is most likely that any one disc will contain several programs. To gain access to a particular program it is necessary to:

A. Know the disc name of the program.
B. LOAD or CHAIN the program from the disc.

If the name of the program is not known then you will need a catalogue of the disc. To get this enter:

*CAT or *.

This will give a list of all the programs on the disc. All of this will take time, and requires some computer knowledge. For the casual or first-time user, it may well prove to be too much.

One additional problem is that, on many systems, the program names on the disc are limited to 7 or 8 characters. Thus the names may not be very helpful.

To remove these problems an INDEX program is needed. Such a program is designed to display a list of the programs on the disc. The names can be longer and therefore more helpful. By providing a simple means of program selection and automatic loading, the INDEX provides simple and quick access to the software on the disc. E.g.

1. Shapes.
2. Tables Practice
3. Number Hunt.
4. Maze Game.

The INDEX should then ask the user to select the required program, by entering the number. Here it should check the entry and reject invalid entries.

The INDEX should then select the requested program and load it from the disc. Once loaded the program should be run automatically.

Such a program is given in LISTING 1, and can display up to 20 program names, each of up to 14 characters (including spaces).

This listing may be copied into your computer and modified to suit your own disc-based software.

LISTING 1

```
10 MODE 7
20 *FX200,1
30 FOR T=1 TO 2
40 PRINT TAB(16,T)CHR$(130)CHR$(141);"INDEX"
50 NEXT T
60 Y=3
70 FOR T=1 TO 10
80 PRINT TAB(0,Y)CHR$(133);T;".":Y=Y+2:NEXT T
90 Y=3
100 FOR T=11 TO 20
110 PRINT TAB(21,Y)CHR$(133);T;".":Y=Y+2:NEXT T
120 FOR T=1 TO 10
130 READ progname$
140 PRINT TAB(3,2*T+1)CHR$(134);progname$:NEXT T
150 FOR T=1 TO 10
160 READ progname$
170 PRINT TAB(24,2*T+1)CHR$(134);progname$:NEXT T
180 PRINT TAB(0,23)STRING$(39," ")
190 PRINT TAB(5,23);"Enter the number wanted: ";
200 INPUT N
210 IF N<1 OR N>20 THEN 180
220 *FX 200,0
230 ON N GOTO 240,250,260,270,280,290,300,310,320,
    330,340,350,360,370,380,390,400,410,420,430
240 CHAIN "prog 1"
250 CHAIN "prog 2"
260 CHAIN "prog 3"
270 CHAIN "prog 4"
280 CHAIN "prog 5"
290 CHAIN "prog 6"
300 CHAIN "prog 7"
310 CHAIN "prog 8"
320 CHAIN "prog 9"
330 CHAIN "prog 10"
340 CHAIN "prog 11"
350 CHAIN "prog 12"
360 CHAIN "prog 13"
370 CHAIN "prog 14"
```

```
380 CHAIN "prog 15"
390 CHAIN "prog 16"
400 CHAIN "prog 17"
410 CHAIN "prog 18"
420 CHAIN "prog 19"
430 CHAIN "prog 20"
440 DATA name 1,name 2,name 3,name 4,name 5,name 6
450 DATA name 7,name 8,name 9,name 10,name 11
460 DATA name 12,name 13,name 14,name 15,name 16
470 DATA name 17,name 18,name 19,name 20
```

Explanation:

Line	Function
10	Makes sure that the computer is in the correct screen mode.
20	Turns the ESCAPE key off.
30–50	Produces the INDEX title.
60–80	Produces the numbers 1 to 10 down the left of the screen.
90–110	Produces the numbers 11 to 20 down the centre of the screen.
120–140	Reads the first 10 names and displays then by the numbers 1 to 10.
150–170	Reads and displays the second 10 names next to the numbers 11 to 20.
180–200	Requests the user to select a program from the list.
210	Checks that the entry is valid.
220	Switches the ESCAPE key on.
230	Selects the requested program for loading.
240–430	Loads and runs the requested program.
440–470	DATA statements containing the names to be displayed in the INDEX.

Points to note:

1. The program name entered in the CHAIN command is the name it has on the disc. The name it is given in the DATA lines is the choice of the person setting up the INDEX.

2. The names in the DATA lines must be entered in the same order as the programs they refer to are entered in the CHAIN commands.

3. In the DATA lines each name MUST be separated from the next by a comma.

4. There must be 20 names in the DATA lines. If you do not have 20 programs on a disc then fill the empty spaces with ***. At the same time fill the empty CHAIN commands with:

CHAIN "INDEX".

In this way, if a user does select an empty number they will simply be returned to the INDEX.

5. Once the INDEX has been set up save it on the disc using:

SAVE "INDEX" <RETURN>

6. As a safety precaution the INDEX should be 'locked' by entering:

*ACCESS INDEX L <RETURN>

Once created the INDEX can be used to load and run any program on it simply be entering the command:

CHAIN "INDEX" <RETURN>

The action of the INDEX program can be simplified further if it is combined with an AUTO BOOT file. For an explanation of AUTO BOOT and details of how to set it up, see the chapter on AUTO BOOT.

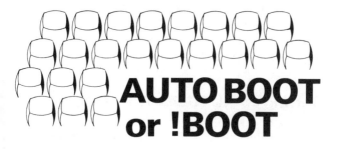
AUTO BOOT or !BOOT

So far getting a program into the computer has required the use of the commands:

LOAD "name"

or

CHAIN "name"

When using a disc-based system, and loading software from disc, a new option is available. This is the AUTO BOOT option. Once set up it can greatly ease the loading and running of disc-based software. It allows you to load and run software simply by pressing the

SHIFT and BREAK keys together. If coupled to an INDEX program this will provide rapid and easy access to your programs.

This chapter will deal with the creation of an AUTO BOOT file, which will load and run an INDEX program.

Setting up AUTO BOOT (!BOOT):

1. Place the required disc into the disc drive.
2. Enter:

    *BUILD !BOOT <RETURN>

The disc drive will be activated and a number 1 will appear on the screen.

3. Type:
    CHAIN "INDEX" <RETURN>

A number 2 will now appear on the screen.

4. Press ESCAPE.

Once again the disc drive will be activated. A file called !BOOT now exists on the disc. If you wish to check this enter:

*CAT <RETURN>

5. Enter:

    *OPT 4,3 <RETURN>

This sets the disc up so that the file !BOOT will be loaded and run on request.

6. Create your INDEX program on the disc.

Note: If you do not wish an INDEX program to be AUTO BOOTed then simply replace the filename INDEX, in the above sequence, with the name of the program you wish to AUTO BOOT.

To use !BOOT:

1. Switch on the computer system.
2. Place the disc in the disc drive.
3. Press <SHIFT> and <BREAK> together.
4. Release <BREAK> and then <SHIFT>.

The computer will search the disc for a file called !BOOT. When it finds it, it will be loaded and run automatically.

Note: If you are using a multiple disc drive, !BOOT will only work on Drive 0.

Back-up Copies

It should be realized that a computer is of little, if any, use without software. Once the computer has been bought the major expense is on software. As you build up a software library you are developing a major capital investment. For this reason your investment needs protecting, i.e. you need to keep a back-up copy of each program. Thus, if the copy in use is damaged the software is not lost.

Copying software is an infringement of the laws of copyright. Thus to simply make your own copy is an offence. At present the situation is confused. Some software producers state that you may take a back-up copy and may even tell you how. If this is the case then there is no problem. If such permission is not given then you must contact the software producers and ask for their permission.

If you do have permission to make your own copy then use the following procedure:

1. LOAD the program from its tape or disc.
2. Set up your blank disc or tape for the copy.
3. Enter:

SAVE "name" <RETURN>

If you are using a disc system then the program will rapidly be saved. If you are using tapes then a series of messages will be given:

A. RECORD then RETURN. In response to this you put the tape in place, press Record and then press RETURN on the computer. This will start off the recording sequence.

B. The name you gave the program will appear on the screen, followed by a series of numbers. As the recording is made the numbers will count the program in. When the recording is complete further numbers will appear and the computer will give a BEEP. You should only switch the recorder off after the BEEP.

4. Check your back-up copy.
    i. From disc simply enter:
    *CAT <RETURN>

    ii. From tape enter:
    *LOAD''''8000 <RETURN>

Rewind the tape to the start of the recording and then play the tape. This will allow the computer to check the recording. If all is well the program will 'load' without fault. If this does not happen then rewind and go back to 3 above.

Once the back-up is made, store the original copy in a cool place away from any electrical interference.

If the above method does not work it may well be that the software is protected in some way. It may also be that the program is kept in memory in an odd way. In such a case return to the producer for instructions and help.